Contents

INTRODUCTION

Sheer joy: Putting the ball in the net is what attackers are all about.

THEY CALL IT THE GLORY GAME

The famous Brazilian, Pele, once called football 'the Glory Game'. Arguably the greatest player of all time, Pele played more than 1,000 senior games and scored more than 1,000 goals. He won three World Cups – the first when he was just 17 – and gained worldwide fame that lasted long after he actually retired from playing football.

His sheer joy for the game – especially scoring goals – was obvious in pictures from his playing days. And you only have to look at any newspaper or football magazine to see players celebrating scoring.

Perfect poise: Spain's Raul about to shoot for goa

Goals – and glory – are what the game is all about. It is not always the attackers who score the goals, but it is their job on the pitch to do so, or to lay on chances for their teammates. Some of the best attackers manage to score goals despite close marking from defenders. Other strikers are more cunning. Spain's Raul scores his fair share of goals, but also often makes clever runs to confuse defenders and help his colleagues to score.

This book will help you develop many of the tricks of the attacker's trade, such as shooting, and being in the right place at the right time. It will show you how to lose your marker and how to be a real team player by giving your pals a chance to score.

Above all, it will try to show how improving your skills can be fun – and help you get even more enjoyment out of 'the Glory Game.'

PROFILE OF AN **ATTACKER**

Football is all about goals. Some players seem to have a knack for scoring them, like electric-paced Englishman Michael Owen; dynamic Dutchman Ruud van Nistelrooy; and brilliant Brazilian Ronaldo. But were they born with a gift for goal scoring – or have they learned how to do it?

Much is down to natural talent. But one thing is for sure – all these players practice very hard every day. I have seen Ronaldo in training. He's an amazing athlete with a sharp football brain. But the thing he has in common with Michael, Ruud, and every top attacker, is his huge desire to score.

More importantly, he is not afraid to miss.

Watch any top striker. He is always on the prowl, looking for even the glimmer of a scoring chance. He is looking for the opportunity to get in front of a defender and get the touch on the ball that will send it into the back of the net.

He might see the goalkeeper fingertip one of his best efforts round a post. But he won't stand there and curse his luck.

Be quick: Michael Owen has the pace to worry defenders.

WHAT MAKES A GOOD STRIKER?

- Confidence
- Good concentration
- Courage
- Quick reactions
- Strength, athleticism
- Speed off the mark
- Awareness

Head down, blast away: A free-kick on its way to the target.

Best foot forward: Being able to use your left as well as right foot will make you doubly dangerous.

A top striker will keep trying until the final whistle – and may strike it lucky as the defenders tire towards the end of the game.

Remember, it only takes a second to score a goal ... if you want to be a successful attacker, you will have to stay mentally awake the entire game – thinking all the time.

SHOOTING FOR **GOAL**

H ere are some drills you can try with a friend or two to sharpen your shooting skills.

PRACTICE NO.1

Mark out a goal six paces wide. You need one ball and two players – one in goal, one shooting. If there are more of you, take turns as shooter and keeper. Have five shots each, then change keeper.

- Do not strike the ball when it has stopped moving – pass it to one side, then shoot.

- Try shooting with your left and then your right foot, and try to vary the angle.

Common fault...

Too many players look up at the goal a split-second before they make contact with the ball, and this stops them hitting the ball in the right place.

> ### GO FOR IT!
>
> **Imagine someone is taking a photo of you. Make a good shape with your body (see page 7).**

Practice No. 1.

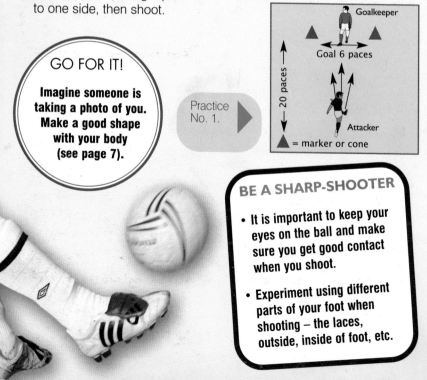

Goalkeeper

Goal 6 paces

20 paces

Attacker

▲ = marker or cone

BE A SHARP-SHOOTER

- It is important to keep your eyes on the ball and make sure you get good contact when you shoot.

- Experiment using different parts of your foot when shooting – the laces, outside, inside of foot, etc.

PRACTICE NO. 2

Set up a goal as before. Place two markers as shown in the diagram, 20 paces apart, 20 paces from the goal. Cones make good markers.

- The goalkeeper starts with the ball and rolls it towards any spot between the markers.
- As soon as the keeper has let go of the ball, the attacker meets it, and strikes it first time.
- Have five goes, then change roles.
- Play three sets of five and see who wins the most sets.

BE THE BEST

Try tricking the goalkeeper. When running to your right, can you strike with the outside of your left foot when he thinks you will use your right? Surprise is a handy weapon to have.

Key point: Keep your head down, eyes on the ball.

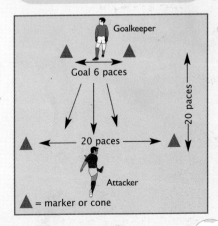

Goalkeeper

Goal 6 paces

20 paces

20 paces

Attacker

▲ = marker or cone

HEADING FOR **GOAL**

Great strikers score almost as many goals with their head as their feet. It is all about timing and courage! Almost all great strikers master how to head the ball with power and precision. The further from goal you are, the more power you need to get the ball past a goalkeeper. However, if the cross has been driven hard towards you, a light glance of the head will send the ball on its way into the net.

PRACTICE NO. 1

Make two goals six paces wide, and four apart.

- Serve each other the ball. Try to head the ball past your partner.
- Have ten goes each.
- Once you've mastered this, increase the distance between the goals – the same width, but eight paces apart.

Common mistake...

Many players let the ball hit them on the head, rather than them hitting the ball with their head.

BE THE BEST

Use your forehead when you are heading the ball. Bring your shoulders and neck back, and snap them forward to make contact.

GO FOR IT!

Keep your eyes open and on the ball – even at the point where your head meets it.

You need power and precision to head the ball.

Time your run so that you can attack the ball.

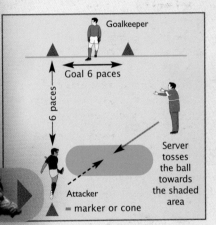

Goalkeeper

Goal 6 paces

6 paces

Attacker

= marker or cone

Server tosses the ball towards the shaded area

PRACTICE NO. 2

You need three people for this drill. Set up a goal as shown in the diagram. One player stands 10 paces to the side of the goal, ready to 'serve' the ball.

- The server tosses the ball into an area around six paces in front of goal.

- The attacker stands back a little way and runs forward to head the ball. The goalkeeper cannot come off his line.
- Have five tries from the right, then swap positions. Have five more goes each from the left. Keep score to find the winner.
- The server must provide good crosses – the attacker does not have to accept a poor serve.

BE THE BEST

Try heading into the bottom corner of the goal, on the side where the cross came from.

- The crosser controls the ball, and crosses with his foot to an area just in front of the goal.

- After passing, the attacker makes his run to attack the ball with his head.

- The goalkeeper is not allowed to come off his line – he must remain between the posts.

PRACTICE NO. 3

Once again, you will need three players. Set up the goal and place an attacker 20 paces from the side of the goal.

- The attacker passes the ball wide to a crosser.

Have five goes from the right and then swap positions. Have five more from the left. Who scores the most goals?

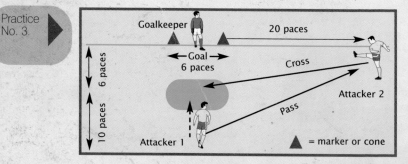

Practice No. 3.

Goalkeeper 20 paces
←Goal→
6 paces Cross
6 paces
10 paces Attacker 2
Pass
Attacker 1 ▲ = marker or cone

RECEIVING THE **BALL**

There are some players who always appear to be relaxed when they have the ball at their feet. Players like Ryan Giggs, Steven Gerrard and Aaron Lennon have what coaches call a great first touch.

It doesn't matter how fast the ball comes at these players, or the angle or height of the ball – they have instant control. That gives them more time to do something special with the ball.

You can develop a good first touch – with a little bit of effort.

First, try a very simple exercise you can do on your own, against a wall, but you can also do it with the help of a pal.

Chest the ball down when it comes to you at an awkward height.

Perfect poise: Cristiano Ronaldo kills the ball with precision. See how he uses his arms for balance.

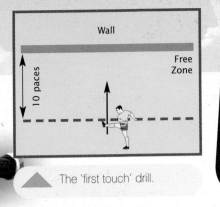

Wall

Free Zone

10 paces

The 'first touch' drill.

PRACTICE NO. 1

Stand one pace from an imaginary line, 10 paces from the wall.

- Strike the ball hard, so that it rebounds across the line, then control it.

- If the ball comes away from you, into the area called the 'free zone', keep trying until it doesn't.

- To make it more difficult, you can strike the ball harder and higher.

PRACTICE NO. 2

You need three players for this. Set up a goal, six paces wide, defended by a keeper. A defender should stand with a ball a couple of paces outside the goal post.

- The defender passes the ball to the attacker, who is 15 paces from goal.

- On the attacker's first touch, both the keeper and defender can try to 'shut down' – or block – the attacker.

No luck this time as the defender clears – but keep trying!

13

PASSING FOR **ATTACKERS**

Passes that give you the chance to score have to be clever in order to trick the best defenders. Passes must be quick – and disguised. Great players look one way then pass the other way, because good defenders can work out what is going to happen from watching an attacker's eyes.

Defenders don't like the ball being passed quickly into space behind them. It means they have to turn and chase back. Try this with a pal:

PRACTICE NO. 1

Set up two small goals, as in the diagram. Pass the ball to your pal using the goals as a guide. Line up opposite each other, with a goal between you.

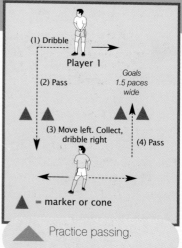

(1) Dribble

Player 1

Goals
1.5 paces
wide

(2) Pass

(3) Move left. Collect, dribble right

(4) Pass

= marker or cone

Practice passing.

• Player 1 dribbles the ball, right to left, until opposite the second small goal (1). Player 2 'shadows' him. Player 1 tries to score through the second goal with a pass to his pal (2), then returns to the start.

• Player 2 receives the ball, takes it across to the other goal (3), and tries to score (4).

• Progress: Player 1 collects the ball. Repeat. First to score ten goals wins. Repeat from left to right.

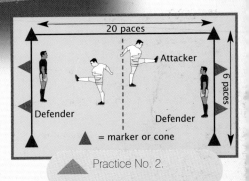

PRACTICE NO. 2

Two attackers take on two defenders for two minutes. Mark out a pitch using cones. Each defender has to protect one of the goals. He must stay inside his half of the pitch.

20 paces

6 paces

Attacker

Defender

Defender

= marker or cone

Practice No. 2.

- The attackers work as a team to run the ball through either goal to score. After scoring in one goal, they must then attack the other.

- Each defender can score a point by winning the ball and passing it across the half-way line to his partner.

- The game is restarted when a goal is scored. The ball is given to the attackers in one half, ready to attack the other. After two minutes, swap positions.

- Try to make the defender believe you will pass – then dribble past him. Try to make the defender believe you will dribble – then pass.

GO FOR IT!

If you pass to your pal, carry on running for a return pass.

LOSING YOUR **MARKER**

Top attackers make space for themselves by working hard even when they don't have the ball. In 90 minutes, a striker like Dimitar Berbatov of Spurs might have the ball for just one minute. What he does 'off the ball' can have a big effect. He can keep defenders marking him, leaving one of his fellow attackers free, or trick defenders that he is about to run one way – then go another.

GO FOR IT!

Make a pretend or 'dummy' movement to create some space for yourself.

PRACTICE NO. 1

Three attackers take on one defender.

• Only one attacker can be on the pitch, along with the lone defender. The other attackers can move along the sidelines, and call for a pass, but they cannot go on the pitch.

• The attacker on the pitch must score a goal after passing to one of the other attackers and collecting the return pass.

• A goal is wiped out each time the defender intercepts the ball. When he does so, he should give the ball back and play restarts. Each game lasts for two minutes. Then change positions.

• The attackers must all work hard to be ready to collect a pass. The attacker on the pitch can run in any direction to fool the defender.

Berbatov: More than just the scorer of great goals.

20 paces

10 paces

Attacker

Attacker

Defender

Pass

Attacker

= marker

Practice No. 1.

16

Outnumbered: It's three against one.

PRACTICE NO. 2

Use the same playing area as before.

- Play two attackers against two defenders for three minutes.

- Rest for two minutes, then play again. Have three games in total.

- To score, an attacker must run with the ball into the goal. Kicking the ball over the line will not count.

BE THE BEST

- Attack (run into) the space behind the defender, even if you do not have the ball.
- If you get free from your marker, you will be ready to receive a pass.
- If the defender gets too close to you, stop your run and come away from him.

GO FOR IT!

Point with your finger to show your teammate where to pass to you. Keep your signals hidden from the defenders.

RUNNING WITH THE **BALL**

The best attackers keep the ball close to them. They don't look down at the ball often when it is at their feet – they know where it is, which means they can keep looking up to see what is going on all around them.

They are aware of their teammates and any space behind the defence. With a burst of speed they can pass their marker – then either fire at goal, or pass to a better-placed pal. Control, awareness and pace make good attackers. Don't just belt the ball past a player and chase it – remember, you need to be in control.

Plenty of fun to be had playing cop and robber.

GO FOR IT!

The cop should trick the robber by suddenly changing direction.

change direction – but the robber must get away from the cop, and the cop must tag the robber.

PRACTICE NO. 1

Two players practice in a pitch six paces square. One is the 'cop' and the other the 'robber'.

- Each player runs round the area, as fast as possible.
- You can run either way and

- Neither player is allowed inside the square.
- Play for two minutes, then change roles. How often are you tagged? Have two goes each.
- After each 'tag', restart on opposite sides of the square.
- Try it once without a ball – then have one each. Keep it under control at all times.

Strong-arm: Ryan Giggs, of Manchester United and Wales, gets away despite being held back.

GO FOR IT!

Dribble towards the other player with good pace, but also have speed to spare, ready to tag him.

Try to keep an eye on what the other player is doing, rather than simply watching the ball all the time.

PRACTICE NO. 2

This is a drill for two players. Use the same pitch as before – just four markers, as shown in the photograph above.

- This is a version of cop and robber – only each player has a ball. This will test your ability to control the ball.
- The idea once again is to 'tag' the other player with your hand.

But you also have to keep the ball under control. You cannot tag a player without having the ball under control.

BE THE BEST

Dribble towards the other player, keeping the ball close, but also keep looking up to see where the other player is.

CROSSING THE **BALL**

It's amazing, but true. Almost two-thirds of all goals scored come from crosses. David Beckham is not only a free-kick specialist, but also 'assists' with many goals. He has a wonderful ability to deliver the ball from wide or deep positions into the danger area in front of goal for his teammates to score.

The pace and height of the cross are important. Anything over-hit could be straight into the goalkeeper's arms. Anything under-hit may be easy for a defender to clear.

Crossing from and into the areas shown – to the near or far post – gives your team the best chance of scoring.

Goalkeepers do not like the ball being played into these areas, especially if it is travelling quickly.

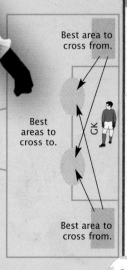

Best area to cross from.

Best areas to cross to.

GK

Best area to cross from.

Aaron Lennon is a picture of concentration and balance as he prepares to cross the ball.

Hit the target: If your shot finds the net, you will have put in a good near-post cross.

GO FOR IT!

Keep your eyes fixed on the ball as you drive it across.

PRACTICE NO.1

Set up two goals, as shown in the diagram, one as normal, the other to be used as a target for your crosses. Put down a few more markers (like the jackets in the photograph) as a guide for your crossing.

You need a normal goalkeeper and an attacker waiting for the cross. Another keeper guards the goal that stands between the crosser and the attacker. If you hit this target with your cross, you know you are putting the ball in the near-post 'danger zone'.

- The crosser dribbles past the marker and then – without the ball stopping – tries to score in the nearest goal.

- Have five goes, then change places with the player guarding that goal.

- Now move this goal and try crossing from the other wing. See who scores most goals.

- This will give you an idea of the type of delivery for a near-post cross – it is driven in, just like a shot.

BE THE BEST

Try curling the ball away from the goal-line, and away from where the goalkeeper would normally be.

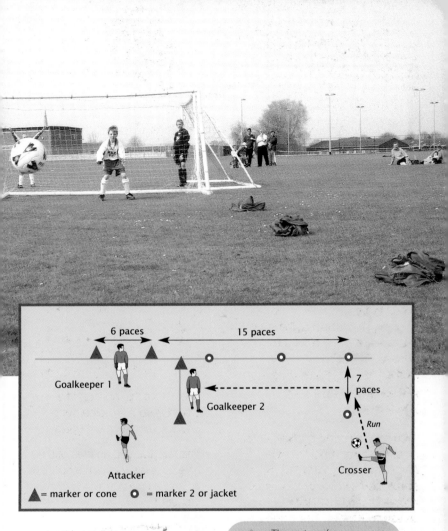

6 paces | **15 paces**

Goalkeeper 1

7 paces

Goalkeeper 2

Run

Attacker

Crosser

▲ = marker or cone   ◯ = marker 2 or jacket

The set up for crossing practice.

Far-post crosses

Repeat the practice, but this time move the target goal back to level with the far post (the second goalkeeper moves back with it). Fire in your cross towards this second, far-post goal.

You gain an extra point if the keeper in the far-post goal catches the ball above head height. This is the sort of delivery you should be trying to achieve.

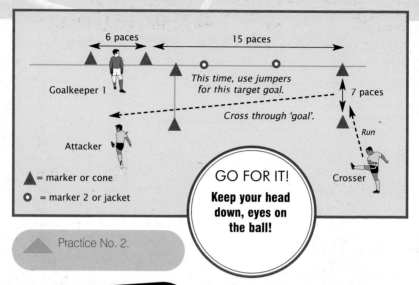

6 paces

15 paces

Goalkeeper 1

This time, use jumpers
for this target goal.

7 paces

Cross through 'goal'.

Run

Attacker

▲ = marker or cone

○ = marker 2 or jacket

Crosser

GO FOR IT!

**Keep your head
down, eyes on
the ball!**

Practice No. 2.

PRACTICE NO. 2

Use the same set-up as before,
but this time do not use actual
posts for the 'target' goal – use
something flat, like jumpers or
tops. This is to make it safe for
the attacker, who will be trying
to score.

- Try to deliver the ball through
  the target goal area as before.
  This time, there is no second
  goalkeeper guarding it.

- Try five near-post crosses to the
  attacker, who tries to score.
  Then try five far-post crosses.

- The goalkeeper cannot come
  off his line.

- Now try five near-post and five
  far-post crosses from the
  opposite wing. Each player
  should have a turn in goal,
  attacking and crossing.

BE THE BEST

When you cross the ball, don't
look up to check out the position
of the attacker in the centre. Just
make sure you deliver the ball
into those 'killer areas'.

TRICKS FOR **ATTACKERS**

Creating and scoring goals is about being clever. Tricking defenders and goalkeepers is the key to becoming a successful forward, like Cristiano Ronaldo of Manchester United, the master of the step-over. The element of surprise should never be underestimated, and young players should practice the skills of players like the old Dutch master Johann Cruyff. All the best players have their own set of tricks. Defenders know what they are, but can often do little about them. Now learn some of the tricks of the trade. Better still, can you invent your own trick?

Clever clogs: Ruud van Nistelroy, left, and Czech star Patrik Berger try the Cruyff turn (see page 26).

The 'Cruyff Turn' is named after the brilliant Dutchman Johann Cruyff. It is a great trick to learn to leave defenders completely flat-footed.

Cruyff scored 33 goals in 44 internationals for Holland in a glittering career. Current Dutch star Ruud van Nistelrooy knows what a brilliant trick this is. It makes defenders believe that you are about to strike the ball, but you actually turn back 180 degrees, to the direction that you came from.

Now you see him... Heading one way, you twist and pull the ball back behind you – leaving the defender on his heels.

PRACTICE NO. 1

Do this on your own, with two markers 12 paces apart.

- Start at one marker and dribble the ball towards the second.

- Shape as if to cross or pass the ball. Instead of striking it, roll your kicking foot over the ball and turn by swivelling on your other foot.

- Use your kicking foot to drag the ball in the new direction (see photograph above).

- Turn your shoulders and hips in the reverse direction to help you to sprint away with the ball in the opposite direction.

BE THE BEST

It takes some getting used to – but the defender won't know where to look! Repeat in the other direction. Attack each marker four times.

26

Now you don't... You can see from both pictures that the turn has fooled the defender. The attacker has quickly opened up a growing gap between himself and his opponent.

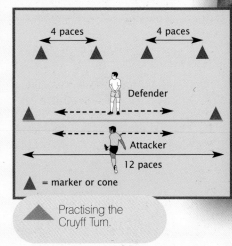

4 paces   4 paces

Defender

Attacker

12 paces

▲ = marker or cone

Practising the Cruyff Turn.

PRACTICE NO. 2

Set up two small goals, as shown in the diagram above.

- An attacker, with a ball, stands facing a defender. Start in the middle of the two markers.

- Neither attacker nor defender can cross an imaginary line joining the two markers.

- The attacker approaches either marker. His aim is to pass the ball into one of the goals.

GO FOR IT!

Use your arms to make the defender believe you will try to score. This is part of the trick's disguise.

- He can only attempt to score after he has completed a Cruyff Turn – maximum of four before he must try to score.

- The defender should shadow the attacker to stop him scoring.

- Play six games, three as attacker, and three as defender.

Round the wall: The defenders try to make the block, but the curling shot is on its way into the top corner.

Can you *Bend It Like Beckham*? The next attackers' trick is named after former England captain David Beckham, who has the brilliant ability to swerve the ball to deadly effect. It is best practised with a dead ball – a corner-kick or free-kick. The aim is to be able to make the ball swerve and dip.

BE THE BEST

- The standing foot must be placed slightly behind the ball (normally it would be alongside it).

- To curve the ball from right to left, strike the ball with the inside of your right foot on the lower half, right-hand side. Imagine wrapping your foot around the ball.

- 'Cut' across the back of the ball rather than kicking through the centre of it. This gets the spin on the ball that makes it bend.

PRACTICE NO. 3

Do this one on your own, or with a pal standing behind the goal to throw the ball back to you to speed things up. Set up a goal and two corner places – each 20 paces from the goal.

- See if you can score without the ball bouncing!

- Have 10 goes from each side; 10 with your right foot and then 10 with your left.

SHIELDING THE **BALL**

One of the key skills for an attacker is to be able to hold on to the ball with his back to goal. This will give his teammates time to get up the pitch and support him. If the striker cannot keep the ball, the attack will break down.

Strikers use their body strength to keep the ball – they spread their arms for balance and to make it hard to force them off the ball. If the defender gets in too close, the striker can 'roll' him (turn away from him and get in on goal).

PRACTICE NO. 1

I call this 'The Bullfight': Two players are needed. Mark out a square of 10 paces.

• The attacker starts in the middle of the square, with the defender outside the area.

• When the attacker touches the ball, the defender is 'live'. He must take the ball from the attacker without committing a foul.

• The attacker wins a point if he keeps the ball for 10 seconds.

Keep your body between the ball and the defender.

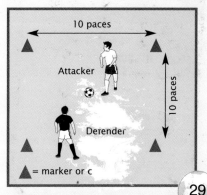

10 paces

Attacker

10 paces

Defender

= marker or c

BE THE BEST

As soon as you have your first touch, turn your body sideways to the defender. If he tries to come around to get the ball, 'roll' him or 'spin' him, like a bullfighter.

PRACTICE NO. 2

Two v one. Set up a pitch 20 paces by 10 paces, with two small goals each four paces wide.

• An attacker starts in one goal with the ball, and the defender starts in the other. The second attacker – the receiver – starts one pace from the defender.

• The game starts when the receiver moves and calls for the ball. The receiver must have more than one touch of the ball. This will help him practise shielding the ball from his opponent.

• Once the ball has been played, both attackers can join forces on the pitch – two against one.

• Have 10 starts each, and then swap roles. The defender should try to score in the opposition goal. The winner is the receiver whose team scores most goals.

Here is the set up for two v one.

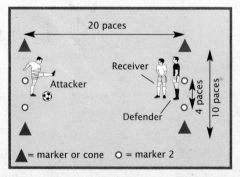

20 paces

Receiver

Attacker

Defender

4 paces

10 paces

▲ = marker or cone   ○ = marker 2

ATTACKER'S **CHALLENGE**

So now you will have learned many of the basics.
Remember that practice is now the key if you want to be a
good striker. To wrap it up, try some of the following exercises,
to improve your ball control, balance, awareness and speed.

1. Frog's legs

- Your partner stands still, with his legs apart.
- You stand 1 metre in front of him with a ball.
- Pass the ball through your partner's legs.

- Run behind him to receive your own pass.
- Pass it back through the legs, then run to collect the ball.
- How many passes can you make in 30 seconds?

2. The chase

- Start on opposite diagonals outside a six-pace square.
- Run two, anti-clockwise circuits with the ball.

- You automatically lose the race if you step inside the area.
- Have three separate races.
- Now do the same clockwise.

3. Head to head

- Use a six-pace square, as shown right. An attacker stands in the corner with a ball. The defender stands in the opposite corner.

- The attacker with the ball attempts to 'score' by dribbling across either of the red lines. The defender can challenge as soon as the ball is touched.

- Each player has five starts with the ball.

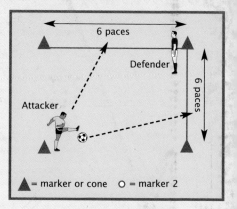

6 paces

Defender

6 paces

Attacker

▲ = marker or cone   O = marker 2

- If the defender wins the ball, he should dribble it across to either line.

4. Head case

- Set up a slalom course using markers that are small and not too high. Set them one pace apart, as in the diagram on the left.

- Dribble through the slalom course.

- When you arrive at the 'passing point', pass to the goalkeeper.

- Then run towards one of the four 'gates', and receive a serve from the goalkeeper. You must head the ball past him into goal. Have four separate attempts, using a different gate each time.

- You have only 15 seconds to score. If this is too easy, agree a reduced time, or add more obstacles.

- Swap over and see who scores most goals.

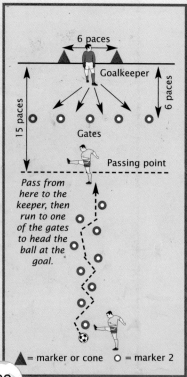

6 paces

Goalkeeper

6 paces

15 paces

Gates

Passing point

Pass from here to the keeper, then run to one of the gates to head the ball at the goal.

▲ = marker or cone   O = marker 2